Sun Drops of the Psychotic God

By

Anshu Patre

Cover Art Design

By Geralt

ISBN: 9798535327303

Dualistic
Universe

The One

Introduction

This book of poetry is the inevitable consequence of years of meditation on the nature of spiritual psychosis. What happens to the psyche when the unconscious overwhelms the conscious with its own system of gravity? What is my experience with divinity and its manifestation in the mind? What is the archetype of the Self, and how did it bring me back to sanity and self-awareness? All of these questions will be answered in the format of poetry and prose.

I will meditate on the nature of mythological structures; how they bubble up from the collective unconscious and shape reality in fundamental ways. Archetypes, or primordial images, are also discussed in the following pages. Carl Jung speaks of the savior archetype, and how it is buried in the unconscious psyche. I will describe how this archetype possessed my consciousness, leading me to believe that I was God returned to earth; the next Jesus Christ or Buddha; destined to lead this world out of the darkness and bring into being a new age of utopian bliss.

I have schizophrenia, but this does not make my visions mere delusion. There are psychic forces hinting at deep realities, personalities, complexes, and archetypes. What truth hides in the depths of madness? Why is it that so many schizophrenics suffer from the same delusion; namely the belief that they are saviors and heroes? What is the collective unconscious trying to tell humanity as a whole when babbling fools like myself proclaim the inescapable and profound truth that God exists in the depths as well as the heights of human imagination? During psychosis, I literally became God; divine and bestial; superhuman and subhuman; all at once. So dear reader, come dive into the dream world; let us walk the razor's edge together. I will guide you into the unconscious and hopefully you will find some brilliant gems in the dark caverns of my mind.

Drops of nirvana fall,

As God cries in heaven,

A single tear enters my soul,

Inspiring me with visions,

Of unity and love.

The acorn of the soul,

Planted within the mind,

Cracking open in darkness,

Breaking into conscious light,

My life's calling is this,

I am a sun drop of God,

The archetype of the Self,

Growing into a mighty oak.

Thangka Mandala

You begin as a slave to ideas,

Chained to the values of culture,

Unable to see beyond boundaries,

Unwilling to enter the unknown,

Then one day you dive deep

into an ocean of shipwrecks,

Searching the ruins of the past,

Hoping to bring up gems and gold,

You separate from the herd,

Looking back forlornly,

Rebels either perish at the bottom,

Or rise to the hierarchical heights,

Either I die in the depths,

Or I hit upon pure gold,

Either I get lost in the unknown,

Or I change culture forever,

Visionary or madman,

Fool or sage,

Savior or lost in history,

It is truly a roll of the dice,

An eternal tree grows and spreads

in the heart of a decaying temple,

The seed of heaven on earth,

Unifying the world in God.

The Mayan Mandala

Losing my mind,

A whirlpool of visions,

The power of dreams,

Washing away consciousness,

Like a sand castle struggling

against the weight of the ocean,

Each wave breaks walls,

Reality loses value and purchase,

The mind no longer attached,

I lose my bearings in truth,

But find them in delusions of grandeur,

I am Jesus,

No, I am Buddha,

No, I am God.

Collective Vision Mandala - Alex Grey

The Psychotic Center

Truman in the Truman Show,

Neo in the Matrix,

I am the center of existence,

I can bend reality with my mind,

I am destined to be a world leader,

Everyone is watching me,

They know what I'm thinking,

Who cares?

I am God.

Eyes Mandala - Paul Heussenstamm

A wonderful world lies ahead,

On one side the sparkling ocean,

On the other a city of golden beings,

Marble aqueducts bring life giving water,

Overhead the sun shining garden,

A stone path through manicured lawns,

God whispers utopia in my ear,

I must obey the law of my being,

Tidal waves destroy the city,

Driving its inhabitants insane,

I build a great white wall,

I know the weight of the ocean.

I know what lies in its depths.

Utopian Painting by Wenzel Hablik

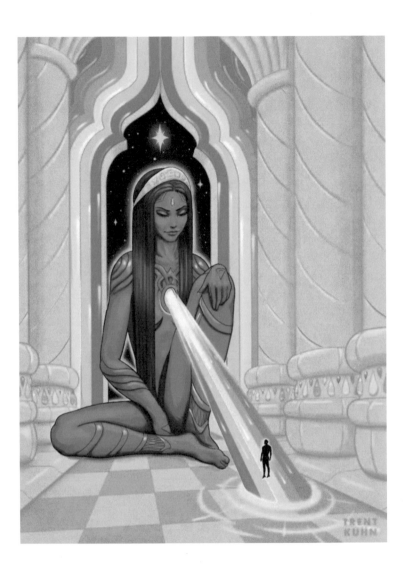

The Anima

In sunless caverns

Of gems and treasure,

On dark and lovely nights

Of sapphire strewn stars,

In mysterious wanderings

Of half-naked holy men,

In cool temple groves

Of incense-laden trees,

Eyes clear and sharp

As ruby hilted daggers,

Arms outstretched,

You call to me.

But I am afraid,

For I know one thing,

If I go on this journey,

I shall never return.

Nature of Mind by Alex Grey

My madness is a gift from God,

A ship of timeless transcendence

in the sea of space and time,

A lone traveler in foreign lands,

where the rhythms of nature

no longer hold sway,

where the sun, moon, and stars

all weave together in holy matrimony,

Where trillions of yellow flowers

float on the ocean of the unconscious,

Only the human mind can break

through the barriers of reality,

If I could share the texture

of my magic and divine visions,

You would believe it too,

I am inspired by something else.

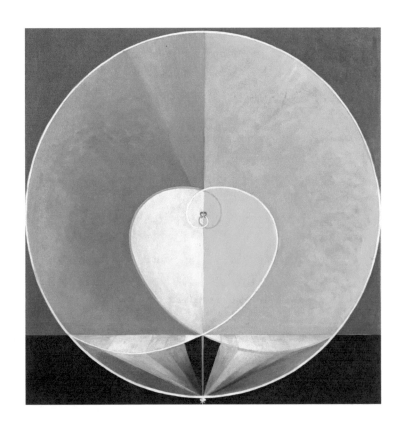

Hilma af Klint

The Hero Complex

Saviors are woven into the fabric of history,

A chaotic force in the name of higher order,

A thread of light in the darkness,

A psychological type, charismatic and magical,

Capable of bending reality to their beliefs,

Delusions inspire the hero to act,

He uses his visions to blow a hole in reality,

Modifying the belief systems

of those around him.

The hero takes an inspired minority,

And pulls them to the edges of culture,

Pushing the boundaries of what's possible,

The spiritual vision transforms society.

Place a stone on a sapling,

The tree grows around it,

Place madness in the mind,

The mind grows around it,

Bent and deformed and unique,

Antipsychotics remove the stone,

But it's too late,

The damage is done,

The gift is given,

There will forever be a void,

Forever a deep dark hole,

Filled with brilliant little secrets.

First Mandala by Carl Jung

The Relation of Archetypes

Patterns of infinite interaction,

God wearing intricate masks,

Someone plays the savior,

Someone plays the fool,

Someone plays the devil,

Images burst into light,

Experiences of the numinous,

Magically creating its own reality,

Archetypes are meaning-makers,

Evolving as the Self demands,

I am going to play out my story

as the fool and the savior.

Mandala in Red Book by Carl Jung

Take my hand,

And let's wander into a world

Of our own making,

A perfect world,

Of white stone paths,

Of golden domed cities,

Of lemon and orange trees,

Suffusing the air with

Heady perfumes,

Sunsets of purple gold,

Sunrises of orange red,

Clouds the shape of cathedrals,

Doorways of light and laughter,

Leading to friends and family,

Feasts of wine and strawberry pie,

Beautiful dreams,

That vanish into nothingness,

When you leave my side.

A lonely desert traveler,

On a starry summer night,

Searching the moonlit sand dunes,

For the City of Fallen Angels.

Of women with long dark hair,

Who ensnare the senses,

Whose brilliant minds rattle

with the sea of a thousand books.

I ask myself why,

Why continue this quest

for an impossible city

filled with imaginary angels?

I build a fire

in the cold dark night,

And hold onto hope,

She is out there,

Waiting for me,

The City is found

in the arms of a lover.

Meandering through

Elysian fields,

You and I

Dangle our feet

in crystal rivers,

Forging through

the mossy glade.

LSD

Flowers dance on little pillows,

Trees wave hello on a bridge to nowhere,

The road bends in circles as I'm driving,

What am I?

God?

Who am I?

The One?

Anshu no longer exists,

Please call back later.

Messiah Complex

God sent me to save the world,

Jesus too had delusions of grandeur,

He may have been schizophrenic,

He dove into the mystery of things,

Lost himself in love,

Then he took a whip,

Barged into a Jewish temple,

Upset the social order,

And got himself crucified.

Be wary of the mind,

It is a prisoner of time,

Spinning stories endlessly,

Solidifying a false identity,

I am a success,

I am a failure,

I am happy,

I am depressed,

In reality,

You are none of these things,

You are not your life story,

You are life itself.

The past is gone,

The future is a field

of infinite possibility,

Act now,

Shape your destiny,

The clock is ticking.

Irrational Beliefs

Reality is a computer simulation,

An advanced alien civilization

is controlling my brain,

These aliens live forever,

Post-biological consciousness

uploaded into quantum computers,

They've plugged themselves

into pleasure dream machines,

I am the dream that

the aliens are dreaming.

I dipped into a future of foreign lands,

Had a vision of things to be,

I saw sunswept meadows of whitest gold,

As far as the living eye could see,

Silver veins of winding rivers,

Stretching out forever and eternity,

The orb-like moon weeps tears of joy,

As you and I merge in ecstasy.

Delusions of Grandeur

God has returned to earth,

Light emanates from my formless being,

I have as many wives as stars in the sky,

And we live together in a castle on a hill,

The laughter of children,

I stand up and go to the balcony,

Looking down on multitudes of followers,

The upturned faces of shining millions,

The sun is high in the cloudless sky,

The City of Bliss flows outward,

Golden pyramids and white towers

as far as the eye can see,

I look upon my works and rejoice,

My religion has saved the world.

As I stumble within

The tangled jungle of your heart,

There are many paths to tread.

There is the well trodden path of day,

Past lush green canopies and clear blue skies,

The path of friendship and safety,

On which many have traveled before.

But there is another path,

Down a dark hole of secrets unguarded,

A path of peril and possession,

Of wild things that stir in the night.

Do I dare wake that part of your soul?

I may not survive the encounter,

With the great enchanting serpent,

In the shadowed heart of the jungle.

Imagine living forever,

Seasons would come and go,

Civilizations would rise and fall,

Our sun would grow old and die,

Universes would expand and contract,

Billions of years would turn into trillions,

Time would lose all meaning,

It is a paradox,

At the end of the day,

Death is what makes life worth living.

The smallest stone,

When tossed into a pond,

Creates tidal waves in the worldly mind,

"He did this to me",

"She did that to me",

Such delusion circles the mind,

There is always this "me",

Always this self-generating talk.

The largest boulder,

When tossed into the Ocean,

Causes barely a ripple in the spiritual being,

"He is only Me",

"She is simply Me",

Truth centers circular thought,

There is no longer a "me",

There is only stillness,

Only being,

Only the Self.

A blood red phoenix soars,

Out of the chaotic oasis of my mind,

An undying circle and eternal order,

Of form brought out of the formless,

Sitting on a midnight balcony,

In the virgin Land of Poetry,

Watching the ship I sailed,

Light up the night sky in flames.

A giggling fool,

Smoking the moon,

Tripping the sun,

Lost in his mind,

As he journeys to the One,

This fool neither knows,

What is real and what is not,

Because he sees,

What is now real,

Can be unmade,

And what is now unreal,

Can be wrought into form.

My delusions are close to the chest,

Rising from oceanic wellsprings in the mind,

They cannot be shaken or given up,

They are a part of me as the sky is blue,

My mind walks on the very edge,

On one side is the entrancing abyss,

The gaping presence of megalomaniacal folly,

On the other is a heavenly city of alms,

The chance to create waves of beauty and truth,

I choose the path of humility and kindness,

But what I choose and where I fall

are two completely different things,

Vision of the Self

Prior to my psychotic break,

I had a divine vision of Reality,

A spiralling constellation of images,

Coming at me faster and faster,

First I see the archetype

of the receptive feminine,

A subtle happiness swells,

Next I see the archetype

of the heroic masculine,

Happiness turns to joy,

Then I see the archetype

of mother nature,

Joy transforms into bliss,

Finally I see the archetype

of father civilization,

The bliss is incomprehensible,

The images come too fast to tell,

Spiralling closer and closer to the center,

And then my soul is pulled out of my body,

Time and space lose all meaning,

I disappear into a void of Pure Light.

Angels with flaming swords,

White horses stamping their feet,

Men in pure silver armor,

Demons with cutting chains,

Black beasts with bloody teeth,

Men in black charred armor,

I sit meditating

between two armies,

As Krishna tells Arjuna,

God speaks to me as me,

Conscious and unconscious,

Good and evil,

It's the creative tension

that makes life worth living.

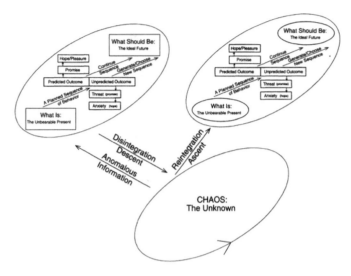

Figure 9: The Regeneration of Stability from the Domain of Chaos

Jordan Peterson: Maps of Meaning

The dawn of consciousness,

Did not destroy the night,

The forces in our primitive past,

Continue to shape the future.

Brute necessity pushes man,

To break away from tradition,

To create values in ossified structures,

His calling is the Superman,

His destiny erupts from the valley,

Soars past the paths of mortals,

To the highest snowy peaks,

I come from on high,

To spin wonderful truths,

Of gods among men,

Creators and inspirers,

Of culture brought up

from the depths of the Self.

Jesus follows his own law of love,

Beyond the limits of morality,

Beyond the divinity of Caesars,

Power and madness go hand in hand,

The universal Roman empire,

Transformed into God's kingdom,

The chaos of psychic forces,

Demands the rise of personality,

A beacon of light in the dark,

A heroic slayer of the dragon,

A martyr for the masses,

Finding the treasure of the spirit,

Realizing the meaning of life.

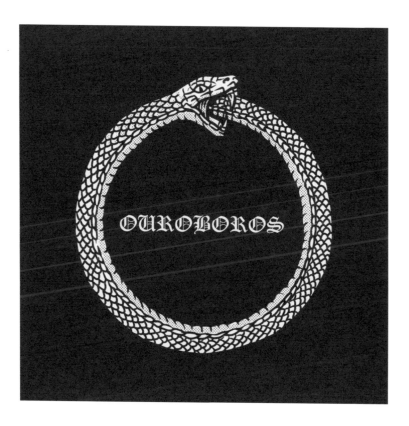

A God immortal seeds himself,

The Great Mother impregnates herself,

Cycles of unity circle forever,

Self regenerating and self-devouring,

The original mandala of all is one.

Being Beyond Good and Evil
Friedrich Nietzsche and the New Age

By

Anshu Patre

Nietzschean Metaphysics

New Age Metaphysics

Introduction

Friedrich Nietzsche spent almost all of his life on the fringes of philosophical endeavor. He did not acquire much fame during his productive years. He published his books and very few people read them. He was sick for most of his life, and lost his mind near the very end. But did this stop Nietzsche from writing? No. Well, the insanity did. But for the most part, Nietzsche kept on going because he was sure that he had struck philosophical gold. And you know what, he was right.

Sure, he was taken up and used by the Nazis. Sure, people from the eugenics movement used his ideas to call for the genetic creation of a superior race (transhumanism as it is called today). Sure, he thought women were cows and inferior social butterflies.

All of this may lead one to surmise that Nietzsche was "evil". I certainly do not aim to convince you of the opposite. Instead, I write this book for three reasons: 1. I am a new age hippie who is crazy enough to believe that Nietzsche can be used to further my own agenda of creating utopia. 2. Nietzsche was, for all intents and purposes, the most *prophetic* writer of his time. He sensed subtle vibrations in the cultural landscape that would turn into earthquakes as the twentieth century progressed. 3. Nietzsche went big. He did not parse definitions and little thoughts. He asked the big questions and even tried to answer them.

Each one of these big questions explodes in the mind, creating connections between ideas that you never knew you had. As you read, Nietzsche has you asking the question: What do "I" really value? Such thoughts are incredibly destructive. If you don't hold on tight, you'll be swept away into this strange universe of impulses and instincts, values built on partial truths, and flights of imagination divorced from reality as it truly is. His is a philosophy of radical freedom; freedom from truth, freedom from good and evil, and freedom from everything that makes man holy.

This work seeks to extend and build upon Nietzsche's idea of the Will to Power and interrelation of opposites. I expand his ideas into my own conceptual structure of the Will to Awakening. I seek to show how and why this transformation of his thought better applies to reality, truth, culture, ethics, and value.

The following book is one branch of the deeper metaphysical root and ontological trunk of my other book, Light. My ideas are slowly growing, evolving, spreading out, and reaching towards the sun. Unfortunately, Nietzsche seeks to cut down my little tree. This I refuse to allow. To see untruth in truth and lack of value in value (or, more accurately, to see the partiality of truth and values) does not destroy such truth and value. This, I think, is one fundamental idea of this book.

On the Unity of Opposites

Two pictures should suffice to give the reader an understanding of the general contours of the following chapter:

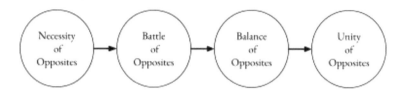

Master Morality	Transvaluation of Values	Slave Morality
Religion	Death of God	Science
Aristocracy	Revolution	Democracy
Higher Race	Will to Power	The Herd
Overman	Eternal Recurrence	Last Man

We humans take for granted much of what our forebears sacrificed so much for. The freedom that I have was won by soldiers on the beaches of Normandy. The equality I experience was created by the struggles of Gandhi and Martin Luther King. The love and social unity that I see was elevated by the sacrifice of Jesus and the Buddha.

But too much freedom destroys freedom. Too much equality undermines equality. And too much love, well, it gets you killed. This is one reason that I read Friedrich Nietzsche. In his book,

Beyond Good and Evil, Nietzsche provides us with a conceptual key that potentially unlocks the brilliance of his entire philosophy.

It all starts with the simple idea that our existence is a dynamic interplay of opposites. From this vantage point, we enter into the complexities of Nietzsche without losing the thread of his central conception: the Will to Power.

Nietzsche starts off the idea of the interrelation of opposites with the following question: *"How could anything originate out of its opposite? For example, truth out of error? or the Will to Truth out of the will to deception? or the generous deed out of selfishness? or the pure sun-bright vision of the wise man out of covetousness?"*

Neitzsche continues, *"In spite of all the value which may belong to the true, the positive, and the unselfish, it might be possible that a higher and more fundamental value for life generally should be assigned to pretense, to the will to delusion, to selfishness and cupidity. It might even be possible that what constitutes the value of those good and respected things, consists precisely in their being insidiously related, knotted, and crocheted to these evil and apparently opposed things – perhaps even in being essentially identical with them. Perhaps!"*

If you consider the implications, this one idea applies to literally everything under the umbrella of philosophy. In the above quotes, Nietzsche touches on culture, truth, ethics, and value. The idea is quite beautiful in its ability to weave together the conflicts of logic and reality. The second you open yourself to the possibility that "cause and effect" do not only operate on one side of duality (that good creates good and evil engenders greater evil), the complexity of history and society is made clear in a simple manner.

Philosophers strive for this simplicity. It keeps the limited mind from losing itself in particulars. Instead, it focuses us on universals; the big picture. But problems arise once we jump into Nietzsche's most important idea: the Will to Power.

"Life is an instinct for growth, for survival, for the accumulation of forces, for power."

This is where things get down and dirty because *power is often a zero sum game in reality. Power, especially in the world of politics, is a limited resource.* Applied to the idea of opposites, this means that the more power given to one side of reality, the less power available for the other. Therefore, power is relational. It is both actual and cultural, existing as both political resources and social legitimacy in the imagination of a people.

The finite quality of power is one reason Nietzsche attacks anything and everything that insults his conscience. He *ultimately* argues for one side of duality. Later, we will see that my central conception, the Will to Awakening, does not follow this trend. *My conception is fundamentally nondualistic because awakening is not limited by time, space, causality, and material considerations.* It is infinite in scope.

But I digress. The Will to Power is a dynamic concept. It is chaotic, but introduces a unifying idea. Everything, it seems, competes for power. Life, politics, values. Truth is only dignified as truth if it expresses itself as power.

"All things are subject to interpretation, whichever interpretation prevails at a given time is a function of power and not truth."

Power is both a feeling and an actual state of affairs. It is the feeling of increase. Power is only felt as such when it is on the rise; when it overcomes internal or external obstacles. Moreover, power is the ability to effect change in the world around you. But the simple truth is: If both you and I exist in society together, and if I have the power to change things, then the things that are being changed may in fact be related to you; they may in fact *be you*.

Here's an example. The more power and freedom the Nazis gained in German society, the less power and freedom the Jews had. Here's a more complicated example. The more power people have to effect change through democracy, the less power that politicians have to act according to their own convictions. Power may not be a zero sum game all the time. But even if, by some miracle, one is able to expand power for all, this often results in greater expansion for some and less expansion for others.

The Location of Power

As humanity has progressed, our species has developed ways to expand power over nature, both human nature and mother nature. But what is the source of this power? The source of human power originates from the power of nature. Power creates power that turns upon power (remember the idea of origination from opposites). For the moment, we will forgo discussion of this process of power transformation in the human and focus on the location of power in mother nature.

Let us face the truth. Nature can be cold, indifferent, mean, and harsh. Every form is subject to the same chaotic law. Life struggles and strives for survival. Animals eat other animals. The weather kills when it gets too hot, cold, or violent. The primary way to describe nature is that it presents obstacles to the life form. Thus, an animal needs power to simply survive, to surmount the obstacles presented by the universe.

But once an animal gains this power, it doesn't stop at survival. It doesn't say, "Okay, now I have the power to get resources. Let me just relax." The desire for survival is the desire for power, and this will, this force, extends itself past survival to proliferation, expansion, and growth beyond limits.

"A living thing seeks above all to discharge its strength - life itself is WILL TO POWER; self-preservation is only one of the indirect and most frequent RESULTS thereof."

Humanity is largely an extension of nature. Thus, applying the same natural law to humans is justified to an extent. It just gets more complicated with us. The Will to Power is the will to separation, to rank, to difference, to the ideal of superiority as judged by power. As humans increasingly go beyond mere survival, power increasingly turns and exercises itself on other humans. This movement of power, according to Nietzsche, is the basis of all higher civilizations.

"Let us acknowledge unprejudicedly how every higher civilization hitherto has ORIGINATED! Men with a still natural nature, barbarians in every terrible sense of the word, men of prey, still in possession of unbroken strength of will and desire for power, threw themselves upon weaker, more moral, more peaceful races (perhaps trading or cattle-rearing communities), or upon old mellow civilizations in which the final vital force was flickering out in brilliant fireworks of wit and depravity. At the commencement, the noble caste was always the barbarian caste: their superiority did not consist first of all in their physical, but in their psychical power--they were more COMPLETE men (which at every point also implies the same as "more complete beasts")."

The subjugation of other tribes and races is necessary for the elevation of humanity. Morality and social unity are not the key to the success of society. It is power. Suffice it to say that I do not agree with this simplistic vision of history. Many complex factors go into the origin of civilization. Indeed, barbarians frequently bring down civilization, not lift it up.

And yet Nietzsche speaks to a deep truth. In a particular context and from a particular lens, power is the force behind civilization. It is especially true when conditions are tough, when war is the way of things, and when values are valued due to their ability to promote survival and expansion. What are these valued values?

There is power, pride, cruelty, egotism, vengeance, nobility, austerity, subtlety, severity, hierarchy, rank, and authority. This "master morality" initially rises because it is useful during times of war and struggle. It is valuable not because it is good, but because it is necessary. It is creative not because the barbarian is the peak of culture, but because barbarians *have to* erect civilization for protection and proliferation.

It is the curse of human existence to act out what is expedient and necessary, and only after the fact rationalize our instincts into moral doctrines. But this process of rationalization, detachment, and observation leads to the movement of value from being instrumental to intrinsic. It is this movement that creates ideals of intrinsic worth and natural superiority. You go from being physically and intellectually superior to feeling morally and intrinsically superior.

"Throughout the longest period of human history - one calls it the prehistoric period - the value or non-value of an action was inferred from its CONSEQUENCES...Let us call this the pre-moral period of mankind...In the last ten thousand years, on the other hand, on certain large portions of the earth, one has gradually got so far, that one no longer lets the consequences of an action, but its origin, decide with regard to its worth...the belief in "origin", the mark of a period designated in the narrower sense as the MORAL one...

This process of the interiorization of value is part of the Will to Power. It is the foundation of Nietzsche's master morality. Depending on how you look at it, the *content, values, or substance* of society is either the result of *structure, utility, and material foundations,* or it is the substance that maintains the structure. The substance is the master morality, and the political and socio-economic structure is what Nietzsche calls aristocracy.

"EVERY elevation of the type "man," has hitherto been the work of an aristocratic society and so it will always be--a society believing in a long scale of gradations of rank and differences of worth among human beings, and requiring slavery in some form or other."

"The essential thing, however, in a good and healthy aristocracy is that it should not regard itself as a function either of the kingship or the commonwealth, but as the SIGNIFICANCE and highest justification thereof--that it should therefore accept with a good conscience the sacrifice of a legion of individuals, who, FOR ITS SAKE, must be suppressed and reduced to imperfect men, to slaves and instruments. Its fundamental belief must be precisely that society is NOT allowed to exist for its own sake, but only as a foundation and scaffolding, by means of which a select class of beings may be able to elevate themselves to their higher duties, and in general to a higher EXISTENCE: like those sun-seeking climbing plants in Java--they are called Sipo Matador,-- which encircle an oak so long and so often with their arms, until at last, high above it, but supported by it, they can unfold their tops in the open light, and exhibit their happiness."

Such an aristocracy is the ideal social structure for Nietzsche, since it allows the privileged masters to attain to the heights of nobility, creativity, refinement, control, purpose, and power. Rank and hierarchy are the basis of aristocracy, and this rank, again, is the result of the interiorization of value; the belief that one is intrinsically superior to another; that one is justified in enslaving another in order to elevate oneself.

Aside from my natural (or perhaps culturally conditioned) repugnance for these evil ideas, let us examine one practical reason for the weakness of aristocracy. Again, it arises from the idea of the unity and transference of opposites. Hidden within the folds of power are the seeds of degradation and weakness. And hidden within the structure of aristocracy is the beginning of democracy.

To illustrate this process of an opposite giving birth to its opposite, we need to focus on the nature of the individual. Let's call him Mr. Fancypants. There are two directions by which Fancypants degrades himself. The first is the external reason. Nietzsche clearly states that it is the presence of strife and unfavorable conditions that push the master to dominate reality. The harsh quality of reality focuses the individual. It simplifies the social structure. It forms the attitude of intolerance for weakness.

Take a look at Mr. Fancypants' great great grandfather. A picture is on the wall of his vast estate. The late and great Master Fancypants is a brute and monster, clothed in furs, with a great big sword on his back. His eyes are severe and cunning. Power is the game, and once upon a time the Fancypants dynasty played the game well.

But today Mr. Fancypants doesn't need to struggle for his survival. He is a dandy. He wears fine clothes and jewels on his fingers. He drinks fine wine everyday and thinks shallow thoughts of women and gossip. He lives the good life of ease and comfort. Moreover, Mr. Fancypants has convinced himself that he *deserves* all of this luxury. He is, after all, an aristocrat, right? Generations of wealth have made the Fancypants weak and effeminate.

When power transfers itself by heredity from father to son, it is quite inevitable that a weak link emerges in the chain of brutal and cunning humans. Moreover, this weakling is not a true individual, but a slave to ancestry and tradition. He does not adapt and cannot maintain power as the times change. He follows the past or the future. He does not determine values in the present, but allows values to determine him.

The Dislocation of Power

Weak willed men are the natural result of hereditary aristocracy. If struggle creates greatness, then the ease of the upper class creates mediocrity. Such men do not take power. They in fact slowly give up power over the centuries, and it all starts with the Jews.

"The Jews--a people "born for slavery," as Tacitus and the whole ancient world say of them; "the chosen people among the nations," as they themselves say and believe--the Jews performed the miracle of the inversion of valuations, by means of which life on earth obtained a new and dangerous charm for a couple of millenniums. Their prophets fused into one the expressions "rich," "godless," "wicked," "violent," "sensual," and for the first time coined the word "world" as a term of reproach. In this inversion of valuations (in which is also included the use of the word "poor" as synonymous with "saint" and "friend") the significance of the Jewish people is to be found; and it is with THEM that the SLAVE-INSURRECTION IN MORALS commences."

Nietzsche begins his discussion of "slave morality" with the following observation: In the face of this-worldly suffering, in response to the injustices heaped upon him, in a situation of powerlessness and inability to retaliate, what would a slave do? He would act out the Will to Power in his own way. He would create values, moralize about an otherworldly heaven, justify his weakness, and get even by pushing these values into the culture at large.

According to Nietzsche, the slave resents the wealth of the upper class, and so creates a morality that glorifies renunciation and poverty. The slave is powerless to retaliate, and thus creates ideals of selflessness and turning the other cheek. This slave morality, the morality of love, kindness, selflessness, humility, and patience, is not good in itself, but the result of material conditions. It is a morality of utility. It simply makes life bearable for the slave. It makes self consciousness bearable for the slave. *What were once indignities are now virtues.* First, the slave uses his morality out of neccesity and utility. Then, the instrumental ideal turns intrinsic over time. Moral action becomes moral thought and this weaves itself into moral being.

But this is where Nietzsche gets it partially wrong. It takes a special person to struggle against the initial dominance of master morality. It takes a strong personality to create his own values and usurp the power structures of the day. Prior to the value creation of the slave class, the slave accepts his inferior status. Indeed, he even goes so far as to justify and believe in his natural inferiority. Master values are material values. When power determines value, the master naturally feels intrinsically superior to the slave, and the slave naturally feels inferior. Power, being a limited resource, implies a dualistic split between master and slave.

Meanwhile, slave values are spiritual values. They are nondualistic in nature, and ultimately unite master and slave. Man is not simply a material being. He is spiritual in essence. It takes a spiritual giant to revolutionize the values of his day and push us beyond this world into another world of peace, love and justice. This is how true morality, which is based on channeling and overcoming the instinctual self, grows in the human soul.

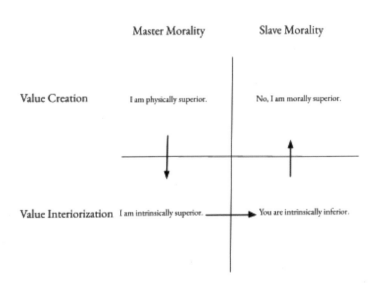

This value interiorization happens on both sides of duality. It is an unconscious social process. But value creation takes place on both sides of duality as well, yet it only becomes conscious when the spiritually oriented slave revolts against the social structures and values of his day. The elevation of slave morality is an example of value creation, not value interiorization. It is active, not reactive.

The desire to transcend the self is fundamental to the constitution of human nature. Humans bond naturally. They go beyond their little egos in the attempt to understand the other. Empathy is instinct for the vast majority of humans. "Slave morality" is a morality arising from the essence of the universe. It is fundamental to the Will to Awakening, which is both conscious and unconscious.

However, I see a more complicated pattern. Slave morality, in principle, is universal compared to master morality. It tends not to distinguish between classes of rank. Love breaks boundaries. In Christian society, both the king and the peasant exist inside one overarching moral framework; slave morality. It is the difference between the negation vs. the glorification of the ego.

I say this to make a fundamental point about the nature of the universe. For Nietzsche, the interiorization of morality has the quality of existentialism; namely that existence precedes essence. First, you exist and act; only afterwards do you think, moralize, and create your essence. Meanwhile, slave morality involves the *exteriorization of one's deepest self.* That is, when it comes to love, essence precedes existence. You *are* love. It is your essence, and only later do you act it out (assuming this essence isn't smothered to death).

This is why Christianity found its way into the upper echelons of power politics. Love and power begin to mix. The human animal is naturally this-worldly (at least in practice). Thus, the other-worldly ethic of Christianity is akin to a balancing. Human nature thrives on hierarchy, but such hierarchy no longer justifies itself. It exists in service of love and the larger whole (ideally).

And there are practical reasons for the inversion of valuations over the centuries. Toil and suffering discipline the slave. Pain implants inside certain individuals the strength and desire for freedom and power. The erosion of aristocracy, mixed with the power of the slave, results in this slow awakening over time. Remember the idea of opposites springing from opposites. Inside of the powerless morality of the slave is the aspiration to power. And within the master's morality of power is the desire to ease the great tension, to just relax and allow for self and class dissolution.

Revaluation and Revolution

Resentment, injustice, inequality, hatred. These qualities are like a pressure cooker waiting for the right opportunity to pop. Slave revolts have been happening for eons, but only recently has modernity and revolution come alongside a significant revaluation of human nature. The qualities resulting in the transference and unity of opposites are as follows:

1. The Death of God - The death of God does not mean that atheism has won. It simply means the breakdown of Christian values and the consequent ascendance of science. The death of God kills the traditional, dogmatic God. *It*

breaks down the division between fact and value, between science and religion. The birth of science arises from Islamic thinkers, Christian monks desiring knowledge, and the evolution of man from ignorance to knowledge.

2. The Transvaluation of Values - A transvaluation happens when a society undergoes a fundamental shift in what it values. Often, these new values are diametrically opposed to the ones they replaced. In relation to the rise of the modern era, this process, paradoxically, is tied to the revolution and dominance of slave morality through Christian ethics. Naturally, the master is going to take the higher ground in the beginning of things, and so Jesus as slave revolts in Spirit, pushing his values of sacrifice and love into human culture by actually sacrificing and loving. But it is natural that what was once revolutionary becomes institutional over time. This means the mixing of master and slave morality. Thus, while preparing the ground for the modern revolution, Christianity also needs to be ousted to see that revolution to its conclusion. This conclusion is the greater unity of master and slave morality, *but with the emphasis and momentum going in the direction of slave morality.*

3. The Democratic Revolution - This emphasis of slave morality is largely the result of the contingencies and necessities of history. Christianity is still alive and kicking. Stalinism, Maoism, naziism, fascism, and all kinds of isms are now in the dustbin of history. Today, capitalism and democracy support the heights of world civilization. Des-

pite the inequality inherent within both structures, they are built upon the ideals of equality of opportunity for the individual. Freedom is also necessary for democracy to flourish.

To understand why these cultural shifts result in unity, we have to acknowledge the existence of an historical asymmetry between the forces of God vs. science, master vs. slave, and aristocracy vs. democracy. For eons, religion and master have ruled through aristocratic structures. One side of duality embodies the Will to Power more directly. The other side embodies the Will to Power indirectly. It takes Spirit time to work its way into human consciousness.

And everytime culture crosses the line between one side and the other, the line itself becomes porous and malleable. Things become blurry, gray, paradoxical, and relative. The unity of opposites and the elevation of a new synthesis is the ultimate goal of history, and everytime culture flips from slave to master or vice versa, or from God to science or vice versa, or from inequality to equality or vice versa, the ideal synthesis is found with greater accuracy. But again, we have to distinguish between the micro movements across this boundary, and the macro movement that now poses the biggest threat to humanity's future.

Why is this Will to Power a chaotic concept? Because power creates power both individually and culturally. It's like a snowball rolling down a mountain. Once things get going in a certain direction, it leads to an inevitable conclusion that requires a conscious force or revolution in the opposite direction. The Will to Power is a chaos of pendulums within pendulums, swinging over centuries or decades from one opposite to the other. Once democracy and equality gain momentum, it inevitably leads to the Last Man, and this in consequence requires a reorientation of values before civilization completely disintegrates.

The Garden of Humanity

But I'm getting ahead of myself. Let us first examine why equality is not a good thing according to Nietzsche. Imagine a gardener who regards both flowers and weeds as deserving of his love and attention. What's going to happen? Well, he's going to create an ugly garden. More than that, the weeds are going to compete, outgrow, and smother the flowers to death.

If the gardener stands for the law of natural selection, this recent modern era has all but destroyed his strategy. Instead, the growth of science, capitalism, democracy, and the world economy has given us a gardener who applies miracle grow and fertilizer indiscriminately to every plant. The consequence is an overcrowded, weed-filled, and chaotic garden. Instead of giving beautiful flowers space to grow, they have to compete for sunlight like everything else.

If you give every plant *equal* care and *freedom* to do what it wants, some plants will band together and smother other plants until only a few species of plant dominate said garden. This is the herd morality that Nietzsche talks about. It is a morality that destroys all higher moralities because it speaks to the lowest common denominator.

"MORALITY IN EUROPE AT PRESENT IS HERDING-ANIMAL MORALITY, and therefore, as we understand the matter, only one kind of human morality, beside which, before which, and after which many other moralities, and above all HIGHER moralities, are or should be possible. Against such a "possibility," against such a "should be," however, this morality defends itself with all its strength, it says obstinately and inexorably "I am morality itself and nothing else is morality!" Indeed, with the help of a religion which has humoured and flattered the sublimest desires of the herding-animal, things have reached such a point that we always find a more visible expression of this morality even in political and social arrangements: the DEMOCRATIC movement is the inheritance of the Christian movement."

Only hardy, resilient, and individualistic flowers can withstand this onslaught of mediocrity. And indeed, many flowers do not reach their full potential because the weeds convince the flower that the flower is in fact one of them (which on some level it is since they are all plants). Indeed, when the flower thinks it is a weed, and the weeds think the flower is a weed, and when weeds convince themselves and the gardener that only they deserve to be propped up because "they have the highest morality", then you get the moral decay, the chaos, and the socio-economic and political polarization that exist in America today. Okay, I have stretched the garden analogy to the breaking point. Let us now continue with our discussion of the herd.

The herd exists because of the human ability to internalize social norms into unconscious habits. The herd uses slave morality and appeals to equality and harmony to maintain itself. But one truth lies beneath all of this false idealism; mediocrity. The mass man has been brainwashed into desiring what others desire, believing what others believe, and honoring what other people honor.

"The lofty independent spirituality, the will to stand alone, and even the cogent reason, are felt to be dangers, everything that elevates the individual above the herd, and is a source of fear to the neighbour, is henceforth called EVIL, the tolerant, unassuming, self-adapting, self-equalizing disposition, the MEDIOCRITY of desires, attains to moral distinction and honour."

The herd animal is a mediocre animal. He is asleep among sleepers. The mass man effortlessly unifies his thoughts, feelings, and actions with his social group. Group consciousness might appear to be a good thing, but it hides the true nature of reality. Social consciousness is shallow, not designed for deep inquiry, and built upon what two or more people have in common; not what sets them apart.

And yet the herd is an expression of the Will to Power, finding its strength in numbers and its leaders in the all embracing State. The welfare state is a perfect example of the victory of the herd. Just let the poor and sick die implies Nietzsche. They have no value. They do not create culture. They do not even support culture. Therefore, they have no value.

Though I do not agree with these immoral sentiments, the point is well taken. Even with the presence of "freedom" in America, the herd is more powerful than ever. Under the guise of individualism, the herd mentality propagates itself in subtle ways such as consumerism and social media.

Facts Destroy Values

All of these forces lead to what Nietzsche calls the Last Man; a herd animal that exists only to maintain his comfort and security. The rise of industry and science provides man with comfort, while undermining his value structure. Think about it. Science tells us that we are smart animals; that we exist on one tiny planet in one small galaxy in one vast universe. Looking at time and evolution, we realize that humanity is a flash in the pan; that we're here one day and gone the next. In the face of the absurdity and apparent meaninglessness of the universe, nihilism is the natural intellectual result.

We're animals. Humanity is going to end. Life is meaningless. But on the other hand, we have big screen movies, video games, comfy homes and couches, an abundance of cheese whiz, and, ah yes, some super potent, now legal, marijuana. It is the perfect storm of issues leading to the degradation of man. Following is a quote from the book, Thus Spake Zarathustra, where Nietzsche describes the Last Man.

"I say unto you: one must still have chaos in oneself to be able to give birth to a dancing star. I say unto you: you still have chaos in yourselves. Alas, the time is coming when man will no longer give birth to a star. Alas, the time of the most despicable man is coming, he that is no longer able to despise himself. Behold, I show you the last man.

'What is love? What is creation? What is longing? What is a star?' thus asks the last man, and blinks.

The earth has become small, and on it hops the last man, who makes everything small. His race is as ineradicable as the flea; the last man lives longest.

'We have invented happiness,' say the last men, and they blink.

They have left the regions where it was hard to live, for one needs warmth. One still loves one's neighbor and rubs against him, for one needs warmth...One still works, for work is a form of entertainment. But one is careful lest the entertainment be too harrowing. One no longer becomes poor or rich: both require too much exertion. Who still wants to rule? Who obey? Both require too much exertion. No shepherd and one herd! Everybody wants the same, everybody is the same: whoever feels different goes voluntarily into a madhouse.

Formerly, all the world was mad,' say the most refined, and they blink...

One has one's little pleasure for the day and one's little pleasure for the night: but one has a regard for health.

'We have invented happiness,' say the last men, and they blink."

Eternal Recurrence and the Overman

The last man is dependent. He is dependent on others, the state, and perhaps even God. He looks for guidance to anyone but himself. But again, an opposite can spring from its opposite. It is the paradoxical nature of reality that even the sleepers represent the beginnings of the Will to Awakening.

Thoreau famously said that most men live lives of quiet desperation. This silent suffering, this feeling of wrongness, arises for many reasons, but one of them is the inability to transcend oneself. And yet this inability is like a pressure cooker. Darkness swims in darkness until it finds the light. Then suddenly, everything that one has gone through makes complete sense. Every event in life paves the way to awakening.

The Will to Awakening arises from the fundamental unity of reality. Man springs from this unity and is in the process of returning to this unity. Even the barbarian plays out the game of unity by erecting civilization and unifying many peoples. Everything is about unity. Sex is about finding this unity on the physical level. Awakening finds unity in the spiritual. The Hindus call it Satchitananda. The basis of reality is Being-Consciousness-Bliss.

But again, I get ahead of myself. Nietzsche provides us with a conceptual tool (if amended) to radically transform the Last Man into what he calls the Overman. This is the doctrine of eternal recurrence. Nietzsche describes the idea in the following quote from the book, The Gay Science:

"What if some day or night a demon were to steal after you into your loneliest loneliness, and say to you, "This life as you now live it and have lived it, you will have to live once more and innumerable times more; and there will be nothing new in it, but every pain and every joy and every thought and sigh and everything unutterably small or great in your life will have to return to you, all in the same succession and sequence ... Would you not throw yourself down and gnash your teeth and curse the demon who spoke thus? Or have you once experienced a tremendous moment when you would have answered him: "You are a god and never have I heard anything more divine."..."

Imagine, if you had to live the same life over again for all eternity, would you choose a life of comfort and security? Or would you take risks and perhaps suffer? Undoubtedly, the mediocre man will choose a life of comfort, especially if he has to live this life over again. The idea of eternal recurrence focuses the individual on himself. It is fundamentally a selfish theory.

So I propose an amendment to this idea. Imagine if you had the power of God and could see into the historical consequences of your choices. Imagine if, once you die, you are shown how your acts altered the timelines of your children and descendants. Imagine that you had the knowledge of this future after coming back down to earth. And then imagine you are forced to live this life over again for all eternity. Such a thought gives birth to the Overman.

"I teach you the overman. Man is something that shall be overcome. What have you done to overcome him? All beings so far

have created something beyond themselves; and do you want to be the ebb of this great flood and even go back to the beasts rather than overcome man? What is the ape to man? A laughingstock or a painful embarrassment. And man shall be just that for the over-man: a laughingstock or a painful embarrassment... "

Only a complete blockhead would fail to alter his behavior and choices in the face of divine knowledge. Moreover, this knowledge would force you to confront this world. You would not be turned away into some imagined other-worldly heaven. You would realize the profoundly meaningful nature of action in this world. Every little deed has world-shaking significance when you see how it reverberates through history.

This thought can provide the impetus for change. It can help us overcome nihilism and the desire for meaningless pleasure. But exactly *how* does one become the Overman? How do we evolve beyond our human, all too human, nature? Here we have two big ideas: sublimation and self-overcoming.

For Nietzsche, our deepest drive is that of power. Some people desire power over others in the form of violence or sex. Others turn this drive upon themselves in the name of self-control and enlightenment. Some use power to destroy. Others use it to create. And still others recognize that you cannot have creation without destruction and vice versa.

Sublimation is the process by which one transforms a drive's proximate goal, while maintaining its overall aim. For example, you can transform the drive for simple sex into the desire for romantic love. Or you can transform your penchant for violence into some heavy metal music. In society, sublimation is the utilization of animal passion for creative pursuits.

Now let's look at three examples of sublimation in the philosopher, artist, and saint. The philosopher, artist, and saint all *create ideas, experiences, and values.* Creativity bursts out of the soul of the universe. Creativity arises from the Overman naturally as the fruit springs from the orange tree. But to arrive at this ideal existence, the human has to *overcome* himself.

If power is the game and if knowledge is power, then the philosopher transmutes physical power into intellectual power. (rewrite) Yet in the pursuit of knowledge, power expresses itself at a level that does not put the philosopher in mortal danger.

One reason for the sublimation of drives is the *ultimate power* that the individual finds in the transmutation. Think about it. In the physical world, you have little control over other people. Even when you exercise absolute control, you create resentment and anger. Meanwhile, the world of ideas is under your control. You can bend and play with them and they won't resist. Blue babies in baskets of bubbles brilliantly burst blueberries on their bodacious bright bodies. See? In my little world, I can do and say what I want.

This is also why the artist paints, creates music, and writes novels. (write more)The artist aspires to possess the power of God, who we are made in the image of. God is the child that plays in the creativity of eternal innocence. This creative play expands consciousness in moments of bliss and rapture. This is the ideal of human culture. It is to create such experiences in the individual's psyche. *Human life is about getting high the right way.*

And finally, we come to the saint, whose power stems from self-overcoming. The saint voluntarily chooses a life of difficulty and struggle; all in order to shift human culture in the direction of higher values. The saint chooses a lofty goal, and devotes his entire will to the achievement of that goal. He overcomes society by overcoming himself. The saint sublimates the drive for power and turns it into the desire for awakening and for the heightening of human consciousness.

"The mightiest men have hitherto always bowed reverently before the saint, as the enigma of self-subjugation and utter voluntary privation--why did they thus bow? They divined in him-- and as it were behind the questionableness of his frail and wretched appearance--the superior force which wished to test itself by such a subjugation; the strength of will, in which they recognized their own strength and love of power, and knew how to honour it: they honoured something in themselves when they honoured the saint."

The Will to Awakening

Alright, I've been hinting at this idea of awakening for this entire chapter. Needless to say that I feel some pressure to really deliver something deep and profound at the end. So quickly let's recap on the big ideas of the essay:

1. The Battle of Opposites vs. The Unity of Opposites

2. Will to Power vs. Will to Awakening
3. Master Morality vs. Slave Morality
4. Value Creation vs. Value Interiorization

So now we briefly inquire into the nuts and bolts of the Will to Awakening. This Will is the goal of the universe. Awakening occurs because of the evolution of consciousness. It is the universe waking up to its ultimate essence through the medium of the human being. What is this ultimate essence? It is God, unity, and oneness. It is the transcendence of self to unite with the other.

As mentioned, this unity is found within the folds of history. Even barbarians desire unity through violence or sex. They seek power, but more fundamentally they seek to lose themselves in the world or a lover. Meanwhile, the saint seeks unity by cracking open the self. The saint loses himself in the inner world of being and becoming. Once self-consciousness arises, humans desire to transcend it or at least keep its ruminations at bay.

Even the desire for division and rank leads to unity because both forms are relational. When division exists, you must be divided against something. When unity exists, you must unify something. So there exists a three part process and each part plays out the Will to Awakening. Human consciousness moves from *individuation to reconciliation to transcendence. You move from the necessity of opposites to the battle of opposites to the balancing of opposites to the final unity of all opposites.*

Individuation is the process by which the slave breaks awak from the consciousness, traditions, and power relations created by the master class. This process of individuation almost always happens within the slave class. Why? Because the values of the master arise unconsciously. Even children act out the law of violence and physical dominance. The process of value interiorization also constructs itself as the ego and self-consciousness develop out of the master's awareness of his own superiority. Consequently, the slave believes in his inferiority because he experiences domination by the master.

But then something quite strange happens. Certain people just get it. They tap into the currents of the universe and the force of human awakening. They create spiritual standards of valuation. Saints feel superior not because they are materially better, but because they are morally superior. Certain people, like Jesus or the Buddha, transcend the material sphere, and yet their actions are all about engaging this sphere.

To believe that you are God and that you are destined to change the world, you must have a certain level of egotism. Therefore, inside of individuation is the reconciliation of master and slave morality. The feeling of superiority is a quality of the master now taken up by an individual whose values are diametrically opposed to the master.

Individuation happens both externally and internally. First, the spiritual giant breaks away from and brings awareness to his or her instinctual nature. Then, he breaks away from the herd and creates new values. But this division creates inner and outer friction as the spiritual leader struggles to cope with the assaults on his being from within (the dark side) and from without (the master class).

Often, this process of individuation is the end of the story for the saint. Jesus went straight up against the masters in control, and he consequently got crucified for it. But when you look at the life of Buddha or Confucius, they chose *reconciliation over war.* They did not fight the "devil of power", but used their awakening to work with the elite. They reconciled master morality with slave morality. They united value creation with value interiorization (if your values spring from the thrust of the universe, they will naturally be interior to you). And they altered the course of history by making the herd a little more conscious.

But I believe the goal of *transcendence* has yet to be reached. So far in history, there has never been a true Overman because you never find a Jesus or Buddha who is capable of wielding power without being corrupted by it. Power corrupts in a world of unawakened human beings. To create a being that transcends humanity, you need to cultivate the conditions for this to happen. And to make such conditions viable, you have to turn the herd into the higher race and the higher race into the herd. You have to turn the Last Man into the Overman and the Overman into the Last Man. This process happens in stages, and by a slow progression beyond all of this darkness that you see in the world today.

I hope for the unity of opposites. I hope that within the last man is the seed for the future evolution of the human race. On top of all of this freedom, there is a new ideal emerging. Too much freedom destroys freedom. It is a self defeating principle. Look at the consequences of our tolerance. Beneath the justice and "turn the other cheek" love that so many of us hold near and dear to our heart, there are Nazis in America just waiting with pitchforks and torches; preparing to burn down everything that our ancestors worked so hard to build.

Too much equality destroys equality. Look at all of this political correctness poisoning our social discourse. When a person cannot stand up and say, "My values are superior because they are built upon the values of goodness and humanity"; when you cannot speak of social progress and cultural evolution for fear of being called an elitist; when you cannot call for the expansion of human consciousness because "everybody is fine where they are"; when everyday people are dying due to the social decay inherent within the structure of American ideals and American life; these are the problems we face in modern culture. These are the issues with equality. We go from equality of right to equality in wrong.

The Future of Consciousness

Currently, man is more beast than man, much less an Overman. And as with all beasts, natural selection pushes us to evolve reactively. I see a future of turmoil for humanity. If it isn't global warming, it's going to be environmental degradation. If it isn't degradation, then it's going to be population growth. If it isn't population growth, it's going to be the end of oil. If it isn't the end of oil, then it's going to be something else.

Rapid change is inevitable. Democracy is in decline. Radical ideas are necessary. And values are going to shift dramatically in the years to come. The question is: which values are going to win?

"We, who hold a different belief--we, who regard the democratic movement, not only as a degenerating form of political organization, but as equivalent to a degenerating, a waning type of man, as involving his mediocrising and depreciation: where have WE to fix our hopes? In NEW PHILOSOPHERS--there is no other alternative: in minds strong and original enough to initiate opposite estimates of value, to transvalue and invert "eternal valuations"; in forerunners, in men of the future, who in the present shall fix the constraints and fasten the knots which will compel millenniums to take NEW paths. To teach man the future of humanity as his WILL, as depending on human will, and to make preparation for vast hazardous enterprises and collective attempts in rearing and educating, in order thereby to put an end to the frightful rule of folly and chance which has hitherto gone by the name of "history"..."

The Value of Values

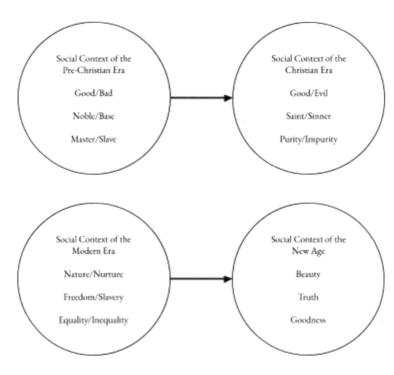

The values a person holds fundamentally shapes the world that they experience. When you value something, you believe that it is good. When something is good, it is worth pursuing, creating, and believing. Humans are creative beings. They bring about what they set their minds to. Humans are also mimetic creatures. We follow the rules and actions of the people around us. Thus, the values of culture matter. They matter a lot.

The values of culture shift over time, and yet each period also has a magnetic attraction. By this I mean that there are battle grounds around particular cultural values that shift only once these lines have been reconciled, transcended, or shifted to such a degree that they no longer hold significance. In The Genealogy of Morals, Nietzsche asks a brilliant question on the nature of value: What is the origin of the idea of good? More specifically, we can ask: what is the cultural, political, economic, and even biological context within which a value structure develops?

And so the theme of this chapter is on value and necessity. I aim to discuss justice as arising from necessity and being about necessity. I aim to trace the necessary connections between various events which give rise to the concept of good and evil. Such ideas preclude the possibilities of much of what both the utilitarians and Nietzsche say. But let's first see what Nietzsche writes about the origin of good and bad, and then let's see what really gives rise to these opposites.

Nietzsche writes, *"the judgment 'good' did NOT originate among those to whom goodness was shown. Much rather has it been the good themselves, that is, the aristocratic, the powerful, the high-stationed, the high-minded, who have felt that they themselves were good, and that their actions were good, that is to say of the first order, in contradistinction to all the love, the low-minded, the vulgar, and the plebian."*

Nietzsche perhaps with this quote gets to *the idea of good as a stable immaterial principle.* This goodness is not tied to utility. It is the result of a deep affirmation to one's own power and genius. Moreover, since truth is truth only in relation to power (according to Nietzsche), and since to create truth is the nature of values (i.e.

the necessary connection between *the belief in* truth and the valuation of "good"), the aristocratic values may arise because of the powerful's ability to push their values into the cultural web of society. But even there I believe that we're stretching the possibilities.

Nietzsche was quite right in his refutation of the utilitarians. For them, good came into existence because it had utility or consequential value. Utilitarians look at the social consequences of acts such as altruism, arguing that such traits come into being on the basis of their usefulness and the praise attached to them. But this view is partially wrong, since good arises from something prior to social value. And it arises from something prior to class and individual consciousness as Nietzsche believes.

Instead, the valuation of good comes into being out of necessity. First, duality is intrinsic to the fabric and structure of the universe. Self and other. Pleasure and pain. These opposites are woven into us before we know what values are. And these opposites connect to the most primary social connection in human existence; the love between a mother and child.

Justice arises in connection to the ought, and the ought is tied to *justice as needs* as opposed to justice as desert. The beginnings of justice may very well have started with women and the mothering instinct. I ought to feed my baby. I ought to feed my wife and children. It is good to feed my child not because my child has done something to deserve being fed, but because my child *needs* to be fed. Justice arises from ought, an idea, and this ought arises from necessity or need. It does *not* come from this concept of the personal obligation of debtor to creditor as Nietzsche implies.

Man has never existed without social bonds. There are many social possibilities in tribal societies. Recent anthropological data tells us that these societies existed in many forms, and the location of justice is different in each society. Nevertheless, the primary bond between mother and child holds and extends itself in tribal societies until, at some point, a critical number of group members is reached and the group consequently develops factions. Or another scenario: one tribe dominates another by conquest. But this is besides the point.

The formation of good and bad does not initially arise from the aristocratic class dominating the slave class. Instead, it partially comes from the *ontological distinction between self and other.* There is a bridge between self and other, and it is only consciously crossed by the saint embodying the Will to Awakening. Prior to this enlightened state of existence, the feelings of jealousy and hatred, the feeling of inner subject vs. outer object, and moral responsibility of debtor to creditor; they all rely on this simple and fundamental distinction.

But the question is: How does this self develop out of the initial unity felt by the child with her mother? Psychology tells us much on the subject. We need not go into it here, but the basic idea involves the formation of ego consciousness arising for many reasons; one of which is the "experience and reality chasm" that cannot be crossed by the self. I cannot experience what you experience. But I can *imagine* what you experience. This point will be returned to later.

On the unconscious level, there are many other ways that the bridge is crossed. The first is the union of self with mother in childhood. The second is the recognition of *necessity* in the form of hunger and satiation. Good is seen in the outer world as food and comfort. The third way is guilt and shame arising from punishment. In this scenario, the self is felt as bad and powerless, while the other is good and powerful. This can mean an inversion of valuation that asserts itself with greater abstraction as the child grows into adulthood.

Indeed, a question to ask: Is value a flexible quality in the human psyche, or do values have a substance and solidity that is resistant to change?

The Moral Subject

"A quantum of force is just such a quantum of movement, will, action – rather it is nothing else than just those very phenomena of moving, willing, aciting, and can only appear otherwise in the misleading errors of language, which understands, and understands wrongly, all working as conditioned by a worker, by a subject. And just exactly as the people separate the lightning from its flash, and interpret the latter as a thing done, as the working of a subject which is called lightning, so also does the popular morality separate strength from the expression of strength..."

Next, I want to connect the notion of a subject with the idea of valuation. Since man is a calculating and valuing being, this brings into existence the *belief in* an egoic subject. When you are treated as a good or bad boy, or when you are made to feel emotions of guilt and shame, you are instilled with the belief of being an individual self. Psychological belief creates psychological reality. Even if the morally responsible subject does not truly exist or does not deserve blame when it messes up, the belief that it does is the cause of its existence. Belief is power. Power is truth (according to Nietzsche). And truth creates your reality.

Many of these psychological processes (the belief in a morally free subject, the practice of guilt and value inversion, the natural value of life, and the belief in evil, etc.) lead to what Nietzsche calls ressentiment. This is when the slave class looks upon the noble class with hatred and jealousy because, on some deep level, it is deprived of instinctual outlets for its drives and may even desire to be the noble class: powerful, rich, and all the other things that come with nobility.

Nevertheless, this jealousy covers itself up in the form of slave morality; the morality of love, compassion, and altruism. According to Nietzsche, the slave class pulls a psychological trick on both itself and the nobility, creating the belief that love and humility are good things, while power and pride are evil.

Suffice it to say that I do not completely agree with this idea. There are many reasons that the slave class resents the nobility. Let me point out the material reason based on the idea of creditor and debtor. The material relations between the master and slave class make it so the master class, at first, appears to be the creditor and the slave the debtor. Why? Because the master essentially gives the slave his life by not killing him. But then the slave must work, and as social arrangements stultify into tradition, the slave feels rightly that he is giving much to the nobility by working the land and fighting in their armies.

The peasant asks, "Why should the master gain from my back breaking labor? Why do I have to fight for their gain?" The masters do not *need* more wealth. They do not *deserve* so much. All of these thoughts coalesce into the notion of justice vs. injustice, and this necessarily leads to the judgment of good/bad turning into good/evil. Again, these ideas do not arise in the majority of peasants. Most people are simply happy to exist. But in the special slave or upper class priest, these ideas are hammer blows on the psyche.

The notion of evil arises when a person inflicts pain and suffering on another without the *need* to do so. This again ties to the notion of *justice as needs*. Raping a woman is evil because the act does not tie to the neccesity or survival of the perpetrator. It is done out of perverse desire. Similarly, this notion of evil extends itself to the powerful almost by necessity, since the powerful do not *need* more wealth, more territory, and more power. But this process of extension and abstraction of evil quickly gets out of hand.

The boundaries of what constitutes evil get larger and larger, and eventually encompass every instance of pride, power, and nobility. This is why reading Nietzsche is important. He sees the danger of this over-extension. The golden mean is quickly lost as dogma asserts itself into the creation of dualistic morality.

Let's examine the mechanics of this over-extension another way. The notion of evil is based on the distinction between self and other; where the self does not care anything for the other. Thus, any act that focuses on the self quickly falls under the definition of evil. Selfishness is no longer seen as *necessary* for survival. It is no longer a *need* in society. Of course, this isn't at all true. One needs to be selfish in order to function effectively in any social context.

And so to summarize, why is there resentment among the lower classes? Because there is *genuine* injustice and sometimes even evil in the upper class. But injustice is a broader term than evil, and frequently the two words are conflated with each other. This ease of confusion mixed with the Will to Power of the lower class leads to the revolt and ascension of slave morality.

The Priest as Trickster

"And now we have and hold with both our hands the essence of the ascetic priest. The ascetic priest must be accepted by us as the predestined savior, herdsman, and champion of the sick herd: thereby do we first understand his awful historic mission."

This section begins with an apparent contradiction: the fact that *truly stable master morality is a mix of slave and master morality.* The rise of the aristocrat is partially the result of domination, as Nietzsche asserts. But what Nietzsche ignores is the importance of benevolent predation. If you're too tyrannical, you undermine the base upon which your power is built. So the trick is to combine domination with justification. You take over the peasant class while simultaneously saying, "Look, this is my land now, but you can work on it and give me a share of the crop. In return, I will protect you from harm and theft."

If you justify, make deals, extract promises, give gifts, and other measures, then you increase your chances of maintaining power. Dealing fairly with your underlings is paramount to securing loyalty and stability. The true aristocrat is not a beast of prey because the aristocrat depends on the lower class in ways that animals do not depend on each other.

Moreover, the aristocrat further bolsters his power through a symbiotic relationship with the priest. Humans are much less jealous and much more flexible than Nietzsche believes. The priest is usually not a champion of the herd. He only *appears to be*. The priest uses God to manufacture original sin and guilt in the populace. This social control device is used to bury feelings of resentment and anger at the aristocratic class. It is used to justify and give divine sanction to the social order as it is.

It is quite a miracle and it tells us much about the human psyche that you can take a religion as revolutionary as Christianity and turn it into institutional forms of hierarchy and domination. People will use any means to acquire power. Even an ethic of powerless love turns itself into power. But this is how the Will to Awakening works. Awakening is the power of Spirit.

But let's get back to the subject at hand. The ethic of justice and love weaves itself into social forms over time because the noble class *needs* the peasant class. To maintain their own comfort and power, they *need* to secure justice for the masses. Moreover, people desire smooth social relations. Friction and fighting do not work in the long run. Instead, you want to instill ideas promoting social harmony into the populace, and the best way to do this is to use God, power, and wealth. You want to erect grand churches to the heavens. You want to build towers to the stars. And you want to awe the people with your magnanimity.

Perspectivism and Imagination

"Let us be on guard against the dangerous old conceptual fiction that posited a 'pure, will-less, painless, timeless knowing subject'; let us guard against the snares of such contradictory concepts as 'pure reason', 'absolute spirituality', 'knowledge in itself': these always demand that we should think of an eye that is completely unthinkable, an eye turned in no particular direction, in which the active and interpreting forces, through which alone seeing becomes seeing something, are supposed to be lacking; these always demand of the eye an absurdity and a nonsense. There is only a perspective seeing, only a perspective knowing; and the more affects we allow to speak about one thing, the more eyes, different eyes, we can use to observe one thing, the more complete will our 'concept' of this thing, our 'objectivity' be."

Nietzsche's belief in the close connection of power and truth is one reason for his belief in perspectivism; the theory of knowledge that says all knowing is tied to our particular perspective; that it is impossible to have a purely objective view of reality; that it is impossible to distill pure knowledge from the values, biases, experiences, and unconscious baggage that all human perspectives possess.

"To recognise untruth as a condition of life: that is certainly to impugn the traditional ideas of value in a dangerous manner, and a philosophy which ventures to do so, has thereby alone placed itself beyond good and evil."

In this quote, Nietzsche traces a profound connection; the connection between truth, untruth, and the values of good vs. evil. There is also a tension between this quote and the one above, since this quote creates an unbridgeable gap between the perspectives of opposing parties because it speaks of untruth as being a condition of life. When you speak of truth as being dependent on power and when you assert that untruth is a condition of life, you make it difficult (if not impossible) to find grounds for the reconciliation of various perspectives. I believe this is why Nietzsche's social and political thinking is so dualistic. There are clear categories of individuals and groups, and these categories have very particular qualities and relations to each other.

Of course, reality is much more messy than his simple breakdown of society, morality, and politics. The boundaries between concepts are much more porous and flexible. In order to more effectively correspond to reality, these concepts must be dynamic in nature. This is why Nietzsche's ontology of power is so capable of grasping an essential feature of reality. When you talk about power, you grasp a vital force emanating from every atom, cell, and life form existing on planet earth. Ever shifting power centers (understanding reality as the Will to Power) helps us embrace the dynamic struggle of politics, culture, and the substance that makes up politics and culture; a certain *perspective of reality that is itself a power center.* Master morality made a value judgment of the world. It is good, and others are bad. In making this value truth (which is power), the aristocratic class created a power center built around certain values effective at taking power under certain conditions. Culture and power are integral units.

Christianity itself is a power center because it makes a judgment on truth (even if it is a mixed bag of truth and lies like almost everything else). It also introduces a radical innovation; the idea of evil. So through the slave revolution of morals (when the moral valuation system shifted from good/bad to good/evil), Christianity became the truth of billions of people (who are power centers) on earth. But Christianity is a perspective built upon truth, and by killing the biblical and dualistic God; by killing the absolute truth of God, the birth of darwinism and science created a power vacuum (created a truth vacuum), which other Nietzchean values filled.

My perspective is this: If predictability is an inherently probabilistic event, and if reality is more complex, gray, and paradoxical than it seems at first sight, then the only type of Reality left after science and darwinism is the Reality beyond opposites. Mankind only has left a nondualistic God in the wake of the death of God. Perspectivism helps us see into this Reality. Power is a perspective. It is a value judgment on truth. This is where Nietzsche's perspectivism is so helpful. Aside from the deficiencies in a perspectivist attitude to reality, it highlights the necessity of imagination to gain greater truth and value through the observation of reality from different perspectives. But this value is good only up to a point.

"That which serves the higher class of men for nourishment or refreshment, must also be poison to an entirely different and lower order of human beings. The virtues of the common man would perhaps mean vice and weaknesses in a philosopher."

The above quote is why Nietzsche's perspectivism is so confusing. If Nietzsche believes that perspectivism requires the integration of viewpoints in order to gain a more valuable grasp of reality, and yet thinks that truth or value is different for different classes, then maybe he believes that some perspectives are greater and superior than others, or maybe his belief in the Will to Power creates irreconcilable perspectives (or power centers) eternally in combat or opposition to each other. One of Nietzsche's most important insights is the division of master and slave morality because he shows us the natural coherence of each set of values. Slave values fall on one side of duality; all mutually reinforcing each other due to their common desire to negate the ego. Meanwhile, master morality values naturally tie to each other because of their emphasis of the ego.

There is the famous story of the five blind men and the elephant. Each blind man touches a different part of the elephant and consequently believes that he has the truth. But each blind man has only one part of the truth. Now let's imagine if another blind man doesn't even touch the elephant, but makes a pronouncement about what it is. Should this sixth blind man even be considered in my attempt to understand reality?

This is one problem with perspectivism. Let's put it another way. If everyone looks at a red block and calls it red, but just one other person calls it blue, what would the verdict be? The blue man is wrong, right? Perhaps not. But the point still stands. The mediation of perspectives is useless in this case. One has to be willing to discount a person's perspective because it is *objectively untrue*. This is the reason that I am writing this essay and offering a different interpretation of the origin of good and evil.

This act in itself, the individual's quest to determine what is true, creates a social pattern of either herd instinct or it engenders the free-spirit. In the quest for truth, Nietzsche chose to be a free spirit. But most people drink the truth from the communal cup. They rely on herd morality, which occurs because most people are sheep; unreflective and unwilling to probe the depths of their being or the universe.

Ultimately, I believe that Nietzsche is like the sixth blind man. The value of his ideas comes from their radical nature. Their value lies in their ability to stimulate thought, not grasp anything close to truth. When you reduce reality to the Will to Power, you make a metaphysical value judgment on the nature of things. When you call different moralities master and slave, you make a moral and power value judgment on the nature of things. And when you say God is dead and we have killed him, you make a cultural pronouncement as radical and wrong as they come. But this is not the point of Nietzsche's writings. He understands the enormous implications of ideas on perspective and reality. And that is reason enough to read him.

A World of Will

The idea of will implies a dualism; a force in opposition to another force. When you have a will, it must necessarily arise and be against something else. But there is another way to look at Will, and that is from a monist perspective. All that exists is the Will to Awakening, and there is nothing else besides this Will.

Why did Soccrates drink hemlock? Why did Jesus risk crucifixion? Why did the Buddha go to all the trouble of starting a movement? For most of history, prophets and saints have risked death to spread the message of greater freedom and truth. Everything that we take for granted today came at a great cost to those who came before us.

Reasonable people would not risk life and limb for ideals and abstractions. Thus, the Will to Awakening is not rational. But irrational brutes would not be able to formulate the ideals of prophets in the first place. Thus, the Will is not irrational. Truth is fundamentally transrational.

Still, this observation does not prove that existence is the Will to Awakening. Look at blooming flowers or the bioluminescence of deep-water jellyfish. It seems that other life forms also go through awakening or enlightenment. Superficially, this is true, but it ignores another truth that all evolution operates with the end of consciousness in view. Reality has the goal of power, truth, and freedom.

Currently, humanity is the highest expression of consciousness, and this internalization of consciousness, whether it occurs through humanity or some species or some alien, is the ultimate goal of evolution. The Buddha is the summum bonum of existence, and humans are a mere bridge on the way to that end. Turn your attention inwards. Inquire into what is. See into the essence of self and universe. This focus of Will is the point of it all. Humans can penetrate Being because being is what we are on the deepest level.

Still, one may ask: If humans are the goal of evolution, then reality must be a cruel joke because humans are far from perfect. To this, I respond: The Buddha is to us what we are to the cells in our body. Perhaps, chaos, evil, disequilibrium, and complexity exist as necessary preconditions for the existence of conscious beings. You cannot have knowledge without the foundation of ignorance. The more truth available, the more untruth is as well. The more good, the more evil. The more freedom, the more slavery.

It is inevitable the first conscious beings on planet earth would end up as the apex predator. Consciousness confers power alongside awakening. But let's assume that it is our primate heritage that causes most of the violence and mayhem you see on T.V. Even if this is the case, even if it is our instincts that create the evil so prevalent in human society, the exercise of power would inevitably corrupt or work its way into the behavioral repertoire of even little butterflies.

That is, even if we came from butterflies, the birth of the conscious self would confer power, and power, alongside genetic variation and natural selection, would create the very same chaos that you see in the world today. The only solution to the Will to Power is a deeper force: the Will to Awakening; the transcendence of the little ego; the unity of self with society and nature; the absolute state of Being beyond time. Imagine if everybody was a Buddha, then this civilization would be much closer to utopian perfection. I believe this is the purpose of existence: utopia, bliss, and peace.

The Will to Power

"And do you know what "the world" is to me? Shall I show it to you in my mirror? This world: a monster of energy, without beginning, without end; a firm, iron magnitude of force that does not grow bigger or smaller, that does not expend itself but only transforms itself; as a whole, of unalterable size, a household without expenses or losses, but likewise without increase or income; enclosed by "nothingness" as by a boundary; not something blurry or wasted, not something endlessly extended, but set in a definite space as a definite force, and not a space that might be "empty" here or there, but rather as force throughout, as a play of forces and waves of forces, at the same time one and many, increasing here and at the same time decreasing there; a sea of forces flowing and rushing together, eternally changing, eternally flooding back, with tremendous years of recurrence, with an ebb and a flood of its forms; out of the simplest forms striving toward the most complex, out of the stillest, most rigid, coldest forms striving toward the hottest, most turbulent, most self-contradictory, and then again returning home to the simple out of this abundance, out of the play of contradictions back to the joy of concord, still affirming itself in this uniformity of its courses and its years, blessing itself as that which must return

eternally, as a becoming that knows no satiety, no disgust, no weariness: this, my Dionysian world of the eternally self- creating, the eternally self-destroying, this mystery world of the twofold voluptuous delight, my "beyond good and evil," without goal, unless the joy of the circle is itself a goal; without will, unless a ring feels good will toward itself— do you want a name for this world? A solution for all of its riddles? A light for you, too, you best-concealed, strongest, most intrepid, most midnightly men?— **This world is the will to power—and nothing besides! And you yourselves are also this will to power—and nothing besides!"**

Friedrich Nietzsche, The Will to Power

What is this mysterious Will to Power? And why does it undergird the philosophy of one of the most insane yet brilliant thinkers of all time? Both awareness and language limit the perception of our inner and outer world. *The Will to Power implies that what is defined is only definable as a result of this Will in operation.* This is true on the most fundamental level. Let me explain. Inside of the human being, there exists a variety of impulses. Usually, these impulses do not make it into conscious awareness. They float in the ocean of the unconscious as indefinable entities and amorphous blobs. They are like a sleeping and many headed hydra. The whole of the hydra is the Will to Power, connecting all of the heads (these lesser impulses) into one overarching essence.

When the hydra is asleep, these impulses (like the drives for sex, food, and truth) reside in the unconscious as unknown entities. But when one of the heads wakes up, the Will to Power makes itself known, and then the human is able to define the impulse that breaks into consciousness. But he does not know that, at the root, this impulse is the Will to Power.

Most people think that power means power *over something*. This is not the only way Nietzsche defines the concept. Instead, power ties itself to the notion of the Good; an underlying force at the found- ation of existence; a directional force of increase. Power is power in relation to itself or something else. Therefore, power is only felt as such when it is on the rise; when we're getting more of it.

And we do not express the Will to Power as conscious agents. We express it because, on some deep level, it is us. Just as the plant stret- ches towards the sun, the human being expresses power as an end in itself. This power justifies itself. It is a value unto itself. This Will is at the core of Nietzsche's philosophy. It applies to every peripheral concept he talks about, whether it is the idea of love, hate, ethics, values, culture, truth, politics, myth, morals, creativity, or greatness.

A Fuzzy System of Thought

Like Nietzsche, this book does not present itself as a systematic attempt at philosophy, building itself from core ideas to peripheral applications. But reading in between the lines of Beyond Good and Evil, we find a connection between my metaphysical outlook and Nietzsche. It is his idea of the Will to Power and that truth is never *being, but always becoming* because it belongs to the *ultimately* unbridgeable individual perspective that dynamically interacts with reality and in time. Power appears as this zero sum game for Nietzsche. The more "truth" and will that the individual can muster within himself, the more power he can impose upon reality. Here, it is difficult to distinguish between will, truth, and power, but all of it comes together to create Nietzsche's valuation of the human being, which shifts from the common herd to the free-spirit to finally the all-powerful Ubermensch.

This structure of thought connects to my own ideas of the Will to Awakening and how truth exists as this *continuous becoming that aims itself at Being.* Power evolves into awakening when it turns on and transcends itself. Truth evolves into wholeness as it matures and transcends its partial perspectives. The relationship between power, truth, and awakening is not something that can be easily defined or made into concrete form. It is all a blur of gray; a process of shifting boundaries and compromise depending on what part of reality one is analyzing. Normally, fuzzy logic appears as a weakness, while I see it as fundamental to the nature of Reality.

A Glimpse of Reality

"The bond between one person and another is forged once more by the spell of the Dionysian...each person finds himself not united, reconciled, and blended with another but altogether fused, as though the veil of maya had been torn asunder and was only fluttering in shreds before the primordial mysterious unity."

When reality becomes an illusion and the illusion becomes Reality, this is the highest expression of culture. Rapture, bliss, ego dissolution, self-transcendence, love, and oneness. If the purpose of life is to reach enlightenment, then the purpose of culture (philosophy, religion, and art) is to create the conditions for this to happen. Culture is the bridge between the world of Apollo: reason, representation, ideas and *structure* on the one hand, and the world of Dionysus: instinct, will, passion, and *content* on the other. Art, philosophy, and religion all take the brute energy of existence, the Dionysian element according to Nietzsche, and channel this irrational madness into the protective embrace of society. These three spheres are the foundation of culture. And mythology is its highest form, since myth unifies each sphere.

Nietzsche was right to worry about the atomizing power of modern culture and science, with its glorification of reason and the con- scious self and its ignorance of the power of story and the unco- nscious. Once we humans started to ignore religion on the basis of its factual inaccuracy, we lost something much deeper than a story. We lost the roots and guts of culture. We lost meaning and spiritual revivification. We lost instinctual power and the ability to transform and transcend the darker impulses inside of us.

Nietzsche speaks of Will being the foundational quality of reality. The madness, loss of self, and intoxication of the Dionysian power appears as fundamental, while the reason, individuality, and sober reflection of the Apollonian impulse seems secondary for Nietzsche. His metaphysics is more nuanced than this simple split though. Hidden inside of madness is the soul of reason and vice versa. Only from our human perspective does the world of impulse and instinct appear to be foundational. Evolution, being directional, has built humanity on top of the dreamlike existence of plant and animal consciousness. These realities swim within the depths of the psyche.

Both meaning and its opposite, both the rational and irrational, both sides of every duality, madness and sanity, love and hate, being and non-being, all of it rises from some deeper Reality. To us, this Being, this transcendent plain of existence, cannot be defined. It is beyond conception. When philosophers say the irrational is the basis of existence, they in fact fail to realize that reality is *transrational*. I believe this confusion is the result of the means and methods that we use to elicit the transcendental state of self. Any external form, from music to drama, that creates "unity consciousness" is by definition *beneath* reason, or Dionysian and irrational. But when one rests in *being itself,* whether it be through meditation or a random flash of enlightenment, then the mysterious primordial unity takes place *in a state of sober reflection.* You do not lose yourself. You find the Self. This Self is rapture and reflection; unity beyond the ego, not underneath it.

The Tree or the Awareness Behind the Tree

"I teach you the overman. Man is something that shall be overcome. What have you done to overcome him? All beings so far have created something beyond themselves; and do you want to be the ebb of this great flood and even go back to the beasts rather than overcome man? What is the ape to man? A laughingstock or a

painful embarr- assment. And man shall be just that for the overman: a laughingstock or a painful embarrassment... "

Where is the human race going? What is human nature after Darwin? What is the consequence of biological and cultural evolution? We look back on our roots and think what? Is our ape-like heritage a source of painful embarrassment? Are we no longer made in the image of God, and instead are an extension of a low, disgusting, and quite silly ape?

There is a simple principle at work in Nietzsche's idea of power. As the Will to Power increases in the individual, there takes place a qualitative shift in the expression of power once a certain threshold is crossed. For example, at the lower end of the scale is the barbarian, who uses power to dominate others. Meanwhile, the highest form of power is that of the ascetic, who uses it to dominate himself. The only difference between the saint and the barbarian is the level of will and power that each can muster within himself.

This formula is unfortunately not sufficient to account for the differences in quality between individuals. And this is where the Will to Awakening comes into its own. The Will to Awakening arises from the *internalization of consciousness.* As evolution occurs, as awareness develops, as the power of will grows, the barbarian turns inwards to become the saint. There is a heightening of internal awareness. One is no longer beholden to the laws of evolution, since evolution is often the mere extension of animality.

What are humans but a higher order of ape? Many of us are just as violent, hierarchical, and loving as any ape. The only surface difference is that humans have culture. But there is a deeper qualitative shift that happens once humans truly become human. It is the Will to Awakening; where humans shift from being the mind and the body to *being aware* of the mind and body.

This awareness is initially tied to thought. By defining the body, one becomes aware of what is not the body; namely the mind. But then one turns thought on thought itself, by defining the mind as mind, and therefore realizing that one is not the mind, but the pure awareness itself. This is the qualitative shift necessary for the success of mankind. Evolution is slowly becoming aware of itself, and thus evolution is moving beyond evolution. That is, the principles of Darwinian evolution apply less and less in direct proportion to the amount of awareness that humanity can bring to itself.

God's Honest Truth

The truth value of a statement depends not on the mediation between various perspectives, but our ability to *be* that which is beyond words. From this place of nonduality, from this level of subject/object transcendence, we can move beyond a world of flux and form towards the absolute truth, which is paradox beyond both unity and plurality.

But paradox does not imply that there is an impasse that logic cannot handle. It simply means that we have to look further and dig deeper. It means that absolute truth is nondualistic, and it depends on one's ability to encapsulate and unify *dynamic realities* without losing Ariadne's thread. It is all about taking nondualistic being and turning it into dualistic thought.

There is always this idea that "objective" truth is solid, graspable, and "good for everybody". These qualities arise from the primacy that humanity places upon sensory reality. We hit a wooden table and say, "This exists! And it is objective truth." But is the wooden table really existent? It is here in this moment, but gone in the next. And so we must consider time, function, parts, and the relations between the table and its environment. The truth of static versus dynamic reality is like the difference between addition and calculus.

And then there is the idea that "subjective" truth is obscure and bendy and "not good for everybody". Subjective truth is good for just one person and does not necessarily apply to others. It depends on the perspective, emotions, and opinions of the subject. We point at someone like Jesus and say, "He was simply sharing his views on God. It isn't the actual truth, but simply his opinion of reality." But what if the individual has access to realities that only occur within consciousness?

To assume that the subject cannot attain to inner truth is a largely western idea. But when the subject transcends himself, when the little ego pops like a soap bubble, he enters a state of being that is entirely the truth. Awareness is the fabric of reality. It is the essence of reality. Being cannot be with the human being. In the experience of enlightenment, however brief, one realizes that Truth is nondual. And it is from this nondual place that integral perspectivism can be expounded. This view holds that perspectives can be fundamentally unified to give us access to the guts of "objective" reality.

So what am I saying at the end of the day? The nondualistic state of consciousness, the intuitive imagination beyond thought, is the place we need to go in order to figure out the puzzles of reality, of consciousness, of physics, and even the meaning of life.

The Will to Awakening

The Will to Power destroys its carrier when it goes untamed. But when the Will to Power turns upon itself, when it tames itself, it is not purely a negative movement, but a positive development. Once power goes against power, then friction creates fire. Every emotion, from joy to suffering, strengthens the Will to Awakening. This Will requires the decentralization of consciousness. It builds itself on the notion that every instinct, every feeling, and every thought operates on the basis of *its ultimate relation to the other*. Awakening catalyzes once the individual becomes aware of this relation. This Will makes itself known through revelation and illumination. Even the oppos- ing force of struggle and suffering (forces that tend to temporarily strengthen the ego and all of its behavioral manifestations) give rise to awakening.

The Will to Awakening occurs in evolution, which is directional and teleological. Humanity (or a species like us with consciousness) did not arise by blind chance. The development of consciousness occurs because the Will to Power turns into the

Will to Awakening by self-awareness. Consciousness provides evolutionary advantages to the organisms that possess it. Every prior will (the Will to Life, to Power, to Pleasure, to Meaning) exists because, hidden inside each, is God and the expression of God, which is the Will to Awakening.

You cannot hate unless there is something to hate. You cannot love unless there is another to love. Anger, joy, peace, and sadness all rise in connection to other entities. The only emotion that has no rela- tion is the emotion of unfiltered bliss. This bliss erases all thought, all emotion, and all experience. It destroys the little ego and opens us up to the summum bonum of life, which is the absolute unity of all existence, of subject and object, self and other.

This unity, the primacy of love over war, is not just some hippie dream. The Will to Awakening finds itself in the general progress of history. Why did the Hitler lose WWII? He embodied the untamed Will to Power. Why did Gandhi win independence for India? He embodied the illuminated Will to Awakening. The logic of awaken- ing is found in all societies and civilizations. Jesus embodied it. The Buddha was all about it. And like a flame, it leaps from soul to soul, from candle to candle, until Spirit has thoroughly ingrained itself into the minds of even the deepest of sleepers.

The Enlightenment of Nature precedes the Enlightenment of Man. Once insulated from the cruelty of nature (an insulation that is the consequence of the Will to Awakening), the human side of human nature expresses itself more fully. The creativity, the aspir- ation to utopian futures, the goodness, and denial of self begins to appear in the social arrangements between individuals.

This denial of impulse, or self-overcoming, is the basis of all moral codes according to Nietzsche. But to overcome the self, one cannot be the self; one must be aware of the self. Thus, the Will to Power cannot account for this process by itself. It needs to be seen as one corollary of the Will to Awakening.

And there is no conflict between power and awakening. This is where Nietzsche has one of his biggest insights. *It is precisely in the denial of self and nature that the self attains to its highest power.* It is a paradox. The denial of self and the discipline of one's lower nature does not smother the life affirming side of things. It simply shapes nature into *whatever one requires of it.* You cannot kill the natural side of human nature. You can only bring it to the light, and ther- eby direct it according to your needs.

Let's put it this way. If Hitler had not taken a bunch of drugs and attacked Russia, opening up another front, it is quite possible that he could have won WWII. The Will to Power destroyed him. He did not control it. It controlled him. And how does one control the Will? By waking up.

Made in the USA
Columbia, SC
06 January 2025